To Capture A Heart

Feeling God's Love

Linda Sprout

WESTBOW PRESS
A DIVISION OF THOMAS NELSON
& ZONDERVAN

WestBow Press books may be ordered through booksellers or by contacting:

WestBow Press
A Division of Thomas Nelson & Zondervan
1663 Liberty Drive
Bloomington, IN 47403
www.westbowpress.com
1 (866) 928-1240

ISBN: 978-1-9736-1415-9 (sc)
ISBN: 978-1-9736-1414-2 (e)

Library of Congress Control Number: 2018900642

Print information available on the last page.

WestBow Press rev. date: 4/19/2018

To:

_____

From

_____

Contents

Finished Pieces

Dedication

To Abba,
Maker of my heart

Special Thanks

To My Heavenly Father,
Thank You for Your gifts so varied:
Happiness *and* sadness,
Joy *and* grief,
Peace *and* turmoil,
Gain *and* loss,
Pleasure *and* pain;
All of them – You use for good.

To Amanda,
Your young mind went where my old one couldn't!
God used *you* to help *me* answer *His* calling.
Where else will you let Him lead you?

To My Dad,
Thank you for being the kind of dad you are.
God knew that who you are would help shape me!

Regarding the Photos

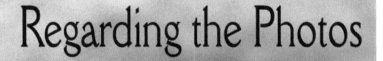

Tiny flowers, mountain peaks
Of Your glory, each boldly speaks
One split second:
A bird in flight
My camera captures
What's in my sight

You bring such beauty
For me to see
Then allow my shutter
To catch it for me
Thank You, Father, for each picture still
For each scene that's caught is by Your will

Seek him that maketh
the seven stars
and Orion,
and turneth the shadow of death
into the morning,
and maketh
the day dark with night:
that calleth for
the
waters
of the sea,
and poureth them
out upon the face of the earth:
The Lord is his name
(Amos 5:8, KJV).

Preface

You've felt it. I know you've felt it! And even though you couldn't put it into words, it was real. And you knew it! An inexplicable longing? An indescribable need? An inaudible calling? You know, those times when there was just *something* missing? *Those* were times when God was calling your name! *Your soul heard Him!* Those were times when He was reaching out to you. *Your soul was reaching back to Him.* No matter what your belief, or your disbelief, your soul – knows – its Maker. It longs to be in His presence. It needs to feel His love. Nothing in this world can satisfy this need. How could it? This need can only be satisfied by tuning *out* the world and tuning *in* to Him. You've felt it! You know you have. Your soul is trying to lead you. Let it!

To Capture a Heart

Here I am Lord, asking again
For You to take my writing to where it has not been
Woo them with words; serenade them with scripture
Paint for them, with verse, Your love in picture
Form the images You want them to see
Yes, here I am Lord, please – use me
Take my mind to that mystical place
Where thoughts, in rhyme, so freely race
Let grace-filled words come flowing out
Instilling belief, dispelling doubt
Shine Your Light through each finished piece
To break the chains of this world, and its prisoners, release
Let every page fulfill Your will
Bringing forth Your voice, so sweet, so still
Touch each heart that dares to read
Capture each one, so each one can be freed

Introduction

The journey of life: the one journey that *every* living creature *must* travel. It is universal; yet unique. It is experienced by all, but must be experienced individually. I cannot take one step of your journey for you, as you cannot for me. But, God has granted us the amazing gift, the freedom, of being able to share each other's journeys. You can come alongside me for a while. I can walk alongside you. His grace transforms what we share into integral parts of each other's journey. Our undeniably individual steps, when taken together, become unmistakably intertwined strides. Our very separate, very unique journeys become part of something bigger. Our sharing becomes our strength. We gain by giving!

Strength, courage, inspiration, even hope can be born from sharing. Fears are dissipated, prejudices are dissolved, and hatred is disabled by the knowledge that is gained through sharing. Wouldn't it be wonderful if you could gain strength from my weakness? Or maybe gain courage from my cowardice? Or even solace from my sorrow? I believe you can. This - is why I share.

My journey over the last several years has taken me to places of extremes. The loss of my mom seemed to mark the beginning of an incredibly difficult leg of my journey. It was as though I had been catapulted into a series of catastrophic events, all requiring me to travel through some very dark, very painful places. But, during this time, I was given respite in places of unimaginable peace and beauty. This time of immense tribulation led me to an amazingly intimate relationship with God. Never before had I allowed myself to be completely still, completely quiet, and *completely* in His presence. Never before had I allowed myself to give my all *completely* into His care. My journey through these storms of life was, and continues to be, a tremendous blessing.

All of our journeys through this life are filled with gifts, blessings if you will, from our Father. Learning to seek them out, treasure them, and lift praise to Him as a result, will make us wealthier than we could ever imagine! The value of these gifts is beyond measure. By accepting His gifts and thanking Him for them, He seems to respond in an unbelievable way! He gives – even more! The only word I can think of to describe the resulting relationship is *satiating*. This word does not, however, adequately explain the vast expanse of its comfort or the limitless depths of its delight. It is *boundless love* bestowing *boundless grace*.

His love is a limitless love, a powerful love, but a gentle love. He *never* forces us to come to Him. He never forces us to seek Him. He never forces us to take of His gifts. But, He *constantly* offers. He continuously woos. He is always at the ready, always eager to shower us with His gifts of grace.

I have chosen to accept that love. Once I felt it, I never wanted to be without it again. My heart had been captured by the *absolute* fulfillment I felt with Him. I chose to seek Him. I willingly, and thankfully, chose to accept His gifts. I believe He has honored my choices. Whether I am traveling through a time of triumph or a time of trial, I look for Him. He has taught me that there is a blessing in everything – always. These blessings can be found in *every* moment. They are there in kindness. They are there in ugliness. They are there in the everyday and the extraordinary. My responses to these blessings: my prayers, my praises, every single one, He hears! Every day that I live I have the opportunity to freely take of these gifts. Success is a gift. Failure is a gift. Happiness is a gift. Tragedy, tears, laughter, and love are *all* gifts. His hand is upon everything in my life. There is a purpose for everything: a greater purpose: *His purpose*.

The following poems portray some of the moments in my life that have led me to lift prayer and praise to God. They are moments that have drawn me closer to Him, moments that have allowed me to get to know Him more intimately, moments that have shown me my complete and total dependence on Him. Some are peeks into sweet and serene moments. Others are snapshots of immense sorrow and sadness. Times of gripping fear, grandiose dreams, and gritty truths are all found along this journey I have been on. But there is one thing that links them all together. That one thing is God's unfailing, unfaltering, unfathomable love.

He has walked with me through spectacularly beautiful times, led me, hand in hand, through incredibly difficult times, pushed me, kicking and screaming, through times of overwhelming fear, and even carried me through some life changing times of unspeakable pain and sorrow. *These* are the kinds of times when God's magnitude reaches out and touches most profoundly.

I have prayed so many times for God to allow others to be touched through the thoughts and feelings He helps me express. He has gifted me so richly! And I want others to gain from these gifts. I truly hope that something within the pages of this book allows you to *feel* Him touching your heart. I hope that the pieces of my life's journey that have been shared will become a part of something greater. If they make you smile, or laugh, or ponder God's splendor, then my hopes will be realized.

Accompanying each poem, there is a verse of scripture. I truly hope you choose to read these verses. Reading His Word is a way of seeking Him. The more you read, the more you seek; the more you seek, the closer to Him you will get. The closer to Him you get, the closer to you He gets! My greatest hope is that in reading this book, you will be able to *feel* His love. Because if you do – I truly believe – He will capture your heart.

Wherever I Am

Blessings aren't always wrapped in a smile
Nightmares happen the same way as do dreams
But You are here with me wherever I am
Whether in sunshine, shadows, or moonbeams
Moments that can take my breath away
Come in happiness, but in sorrow too
Beginnings and endings both come by Your hand
Yes, both must be allowed by You
Tears come from joy the same as from pain
Both water the growth that You've started
You were there in the joy of the loves that I've gained
As well as in the pain when loves departed

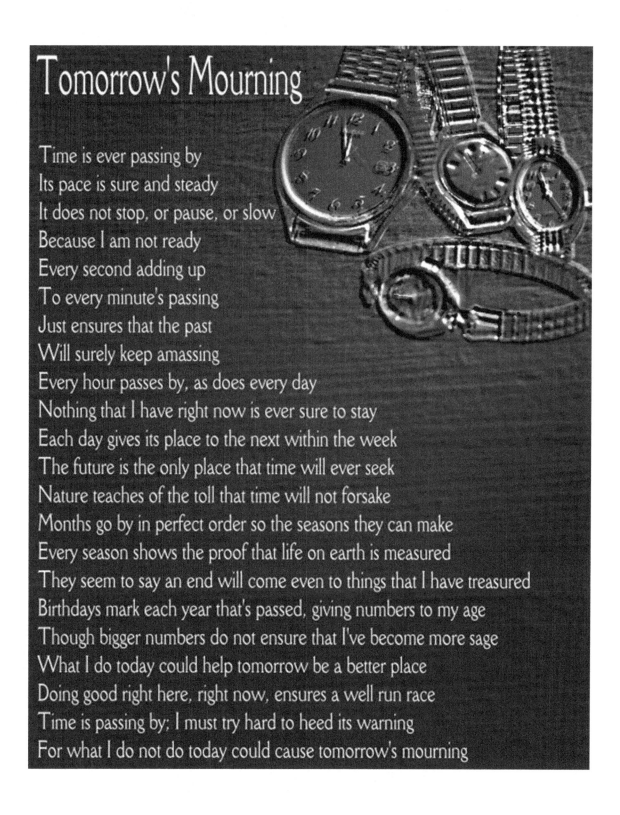

Tomorrow's Mourning

Time is ever passing by
Its pace is sure and steady
It does not stop, or pause, or slow
Because I am not ready
Every second adding up
To every minute's passing
Just ensures that the past
Will surely keep amassing
Every hour passes by, as does every day
Nothing that I have right now is ever sure to stay
Each day gives its place to the next within the week
The future is the only place that time will ever seek
Nature teaches of the toll that time will not forsake
Months go by in perfect order so the seasons they can make
Every season shows the proof that life on earth is measured
They seem to say an end will come even to things that I have treasured
Birthdays mark each year that's passed, giving numbers to my age
Though bigger numbers do not ensure that I've become more sage
What I do today could help tomorrow be a better place
Doing good right here, right now, ensures a well run race
Time is passing by; I must try hard to heed its warning
For what I do not do today could cause tomorrow's mourning

Prologue

What exactly is the heart? I was actually kind of surprised at the definition I found in the dictionary. But after reading what it had to say, I decided I needed to try to define what I believe it is … in me. My heart is the very core of *me*. It is the epicenter of everything that makes me the person I am. It is the source of all my other attributes. It is where my beliefs are believed, my values are valued, and my conscience is conscious. It is the most sincere, most truthful, and most honest part of me. It is the direction of my mind, the design of my soul, and the den of my spirit. It is where my love is born, carried, felt, and cherished. It - is the very definition - of - who - I am. It is what makes me … *me*. It is a beautifully unfinished tapestry intricately woven with the threads of my own unique being.

So then, what does it mean for a heart to be captured? Well, picture your heart as a tapestry. When your heart has been captured, someone or something has, for lack of a better word, *touched* it. That someone or something has transferred some of its own colors and textures to your heart's threads. The very fibers that make up *that* place get changed. Then, these fibers, these threads, get carefully woven into your heart's ever-changing, ever-expanding tapestry. Every time a heart is captured, its tapestry is changed. Its fibers take on more color. Its details become more intricate. Its patterns emerge more clearly. A kaleidoscope of colors gets woven into an ever-changing, ever-growing, ever-more-beautiful, divine design: a *God-given masterpiece*. The heart: the essence, the core, the whole of the person; is forever changed. I cannot think of anything more powerful.

If you have ever been blessed enough to look into the face of your newborn baby for the first time, you have *felt* the weaving of threads into your tapestry. If you have ever held the frail and motionless hand of a dying loved one, you have *felt* the unbelievable strength of its threads; you have *felt* the undeniable power your tapestry portrays. This strength, this power, held in the fabric of a captured heart, is far beyond even the deepest human understanding.

If you have ever tried to explain *why* you love someone, you know what I mean. Words always seem to fall short when trying to describe this one particular thing. Love's magnetic pull surpasses scientific or theoretical explanation. Its magical bond defies the laws of common sense. Its colors and textures are invisible, but yet, so very real. It is a majestic phenomenon of inexplicable proportions. Yet, most every heart feels an instinctual calling, an inherent need, to feel it, to keep it, to share it, to express it. It seems only fitting then that God would use this, the grandest of all things, as His way to secure *our* relationship with *Him*. He has loved us from long before we were ever born. His love for us was the sole reason Christ endured the cross. The Son of God was given as a sacrifice so that *we* could be secured an eternity with *Him*. He not only possesses the greatest love – He *is* the greatest love!

This God: The Maker of the Universe, The All Powerful, God Almighty, the Creator of Heaven and Hell; this God, *this very same God*, gently placed within the hearts of each and every one of us the single most powerful thing ever known to man. Yet, He never, ever, forces Himself on us. He could have just as easily placed a love *just for Him* inside our hearts! But He didn't. He could have ensured that all our tapestries look exactly alike! But He didn't. He loves us enough *not* to force us. He loves us enough to let us choose. He chose to give us the ability to experience loving *and* being loved by others. And He chose to give us the freedom – to love Him. He *gave* us the thread *and* the loom *and* the ability to weave, yet He did not force us to include Him in our tapestries! I believe this is because the inclusion of freedom is what gives the thread its unparalleled strength and beauty. He deeply desires a closer relationship with us. But He does not force; He frees. He does not coerce; He courts. He does not warrant; He woos.

Let me try to do justice to the contrast. The power in a lightening bolt is given by His hand. The force of a hurricane is given by His hand. The might of a volcano is given by His hand! Yet, He softly, gently, tenderly pursues us. The boom of thunder is given by Him. The roar of the ocean is given by Him! Yet He merely whispers our names. The pristine blue of a cloudless sky, the power-packed red of a brilliant sunset, and the perfectly pure white of a pillowy cloud are *all* colored by Him. Yet He gives us the power to choose *and* change the colors within our tapestries. His love for us defies human intellect! There is just no word that can explain it. No definition can reach its meaning. No theory can encompass it. It is simply too big to be contained, too deep to be measured, and too grand to be described. Still, I simply must try.

I have *felt* His love. I have felt it in the kiss of morning sunlight on my face. I have felt it in the lapping of warm ocean waves onto my toes and the brush of a soft summer breeze against my skin. I have *seen* His adoration. I have seen it in the delicate petals of tiny wildflowers. I have seen it in the brilliant glow of a glittering star and in the crystalline masterpiece of a frost covered surface. I have *heard* His whisper. It was there in the quiet coo of the mourning dove and in the gentle spring wind through the trees. It was there, so quiet, so precious, in the breath of my sleeping children. I have *sensed* His care. It was there in the soft sweetness of my mother's kiss and in the strong security of my father's embrace. It was there in the hearts and hugs of all those people who have *shared* my tears and laughter. At any given moment, in any given place, if I look, if I listen, if I feel, I *can* find Him.

There is *nothing* bigger. There is *nothing* better. There is *nothing* more fulfilling. The most intense and satisfying love you have ever felt for another human being cannot even begin to skim the surface of just how amazing His love is. If I could be granted just one wish, it would be that every single person on the face of this great earth – *feel* – His love. Why? Because *it* is what every single person on the face of this great planet yearns for. Most don't even know that this is what they are searching for! They may think that if they get *that* job, or marry *that* person, or have *that* much money they will be satisfied. But, it is actually God's love that their hearts are hungry for. It is God's love that their souls yearn for. Their thread, their looms, their tapestries are aching to be touched – by their Maker.

The Flight of My Spirit

How is it my feet can be firm on the ground
While my spirit soars so far above?
It's lifted on high
Touching the sky
Swept up by Your amazing love
How is it I can be in the valley below
And yet feel my heart so lifted?
It's riding the breeze
At peace and at ease
By Your love, I have been gifted
How is it my troubles can bind my hands
Still my soul flies freely on?
It's aloft on the wind
You constantly tend
It's the wings of Your love that I don

For he satisfieth the longing soul,
and filleth the hungry soul with goodness.

(Psalm 107:9, KJV).

Breathe In the Wind

Think of the times you have felt the wind
As it kissed your face and softly brushed your skin
Think of the times you have felt its flair
As it played so freely with strands of your hair
Think of the times you've breathed it in deep
Hoping its freshness to somehow keep
Think of the times it quieted your spirit
As, through the pines, you could so easily hear it
Think of the times it made the leaves dance
Or made the trees sway as if by musical trance
Think of the times the wind has prevailed
Now, think of that wind – as the breath He exhaled
God's holy breath! Oh, can't you feel it?
No power, no force, in no way, can conceal it
The very same breath that breathed life into Adam
Is the air that we breathe … truly magical to fathom
Your heart can only beat for just a few minutes
If the power of His breath is not found within it
Breathe in the wind; oh, breathe it in
Let it fill you with life again and again

And the Lord God formed man of the dust of the ground, and breathed into his nostrils the breath of life; and man became a living soul.

(Genesis 2:7, KJV).

A Clean-Slate Day

As the sun starts to glimpse up over the trees
There's a clean-slate day ahead
There's no spot or blemish yet to see
As I rise up from my bed
No matter what this day may hold
Or what troubles may come my way
I have a Helper to see me through
He is at my side to stay
Such deep felt peace fills my heart
Just from knowing that He is there
A smile instantly comes 'cross my face
As I feel His constant care
This brand new day now dawning
Holds promise I look forward to
As I walk – with Him – through today
There is nothing that I cannot do

It is of the Lord's mercies that we are not consumed, because his compassions fail not. They are new every morning: great is thy faithfulness.

(Lamentations 3:22-23, KJV).

That's the Magic

As the bright spring sun begins to fade
And a light evening dew starts to fall
The birds are still singing their praises to You
I watch silently … in absolute awe
Every creature still stirring cries aloud of Your love
In thankful notes, their voices they lift
The beauty beheld in this precious moment
Sets time afloat in a tranquil drift
Every sound that they make rings only of truth
They care not to pretend anything
They sing what it is that they feel in their hearts
That's the magic in the songs that they sing

Sing unto him, sing psalms unto him: talk ye of all his wondrous works.

(Psalm 105:2, KJV).

Start of Day

Here in the stillness of early morning's dark
Before the first song of the dove or meadowlark
I rise, alone, to meet with my King
My soul, my spirit, my all, I bring
I open His Word; it is here that I seek
It is here He makes strong what in me He finds weak
I ask for His guidance; for His help, I pray
I ask He stay with me throughout the coming day
It's approaching so quickly: that busy, hurried pace
Where I'll so desperately need His favor, His grace
So here, in the stillness, I will meet with my King
Here, in the darkness, long before the birds sing

The Offering Plate

The birds are singing before day breaks
Though it is too dark to see
They cannot fly, or feed, or frolic
Their song, surely a tithe to Thee
From their nests within the branches
They voice their gratitude
To their Maker, whom they know
Will fill them with daily food
Much like the birds, I awake
Long before sunrise
I sit in the light of my trusty lamp
With Your Word before my eyes
From a chair within my home
My heart lifts gratitude
To my Maker, Whom I know
Will fill me with soulful food
I cannot stop my joyous smile
As I soak in their songs of praise
No more heavenly way have I ever found
To start my earthly days
My heart is filled; my cup runs over
My soul is truly sate
What a blessing it is to witness the fill
Of nature's offering plate

The Weeping Woman

Dropping to her knees, silently, she wept
Awakened in her was all that had slept
Abandoned, discarded, were all her pretenses
Alive, again, were her soul's tender senses
Tears poured forth from deep within
For Light had come to live where darkness had been
She held nothing back; she gave Him her all
Her deepest desire was to answer His call
With her every teardrop, she washed His feet
In this humble service, she found solace so sweet
Drying them off with the strands of her hair
She had never felt love … like she felt it there
Belief made her come, her steps driven by need
Surrender made her kneel; adoration, her tears freed
Love and gratitude and devotion all took part
But there at the center – was her captured heart
This is what Christ saw as He looked past her behavior
He saw what she felt: her faith in her Savior

Wherefore I say unto thee, Her sins, which are many, are forgiven; for she loved much: but to whom little is forgiven, the same loveth little.

(Luke 7:47, KJV).

To See What's Spoken

How could I even try to explain just how amazing You truly are?
What could possibly convince the lost that You are here, and not only afar?
Could I tell them of all the gentle kisses that You send with the morning sun
And of the postcards that You paint just at the time each day is done?
Could I tell them of all Your tender hugs wrapping 'round me with the wind
And of the serenades that through the songbirds You sweetly send?
Could I tell them of the special way You hold me tight when I am scared
And of the depths of Your love for me even when my truths are bared?
Could I speak of all those precious gifts that You give in family ties
And of all the clouded masterpieces that You send across the skies?
Could I tell them of the way You wrap all Your gifts so carefully
And that if they'd look at a flower's bud, it's Your care they'd surely see?
Could I tell them of the promised future You have waiting to unfold
And of Your lasting sign of love in the rainbow, bright and bold?
Could I tell them of Your greatest gift: the *giving* of *Your* Son
And that, through this gift, it is *their* freedom that has so graciously been won?
Could I tell them, with Your help, that You are real and You are here?
Oh, could I tell them, with Your help, so they could see what they would hear?

Come and see what God has done, how
awesome His works in man's behalf!

(Psalm 66:5, NIV).

I Found You

Within the sadness of my tears
Within the chill of all my fears
Within the shame of every jeer
Your love was there; it was sincere
Within the laughs of happy times
Within the strength of youth and prime
Within the awe of the sublime
You have been my song and rhyme
Within the dark and painful way
Within the shearing and the fray
Within the costs I've had to pay
You have been my hope and stay
Within each thing that I've went through
Within each feeling and heartbeat too
Within each breath I ever drew
You were there - yes, all of You

The Lord confides in those who fear him; he makes his covenant known to them.

(Psalm 25:14, NIV).

Nature's Pew

My earthly body feels heavenly things
When my earthly ears can hear
A cardinal as he boldly sings
To the One he holds so dear
My earthly body feels heavenly things
When my earthly eyes can see
The worship creation always brings
To point us all to Thee
My earthly body feels heavenly things
When my senses are tuned to You
My earthbound soul finds heavenly wings
When I sit on nature's pew

Even the sparrow has found a home, and the swallow a nest for herself, where she may have her young – a place near your altar, O Lord Almighty, my King and my God.

(Psalm 84:3, NIV).

One Moment's Gift

Trickling waters in the brooks

Wind sounds through tall trees

Singing birds in branch-bound nooks

Ready to rise upon the breeze

Dew drops falling from where they lay

Spring scents aloft and floating

Brand new morning, brand new day

How I love Your gentle doting

Not one word can I speak

For I am overcome with bliss

My smile reaches cheek to cheek

Feeling You here in all of this

Paradise Found

I have the ability to speak and to write
All the words that tell all my stories
But I find only lack when I try to explain
God's essence, His love, His glory
I have found no words: no, not even one
That can tell what it is that I know
This knowledge is found in the depth of my being
From my spirit, it springs forth; it flows
My soul shares its joy with my heart and mind
In the unspeakable beauty it sees
Wordless praises course through my veins
As silent worship brings my thoughts to their knees
Paradise, I am sure, exists deep within
Where God dwells can be nothing less
This invisible world in which my soul lives
Of its splendor, no words can profess

Branded Hearts

If it were to be possible
I would create with words – a fire
This fire would burn onto every heart
A branding of true desire
Then every heart branded as such
Would rest not all their days
Striving always to have Him fill
Their souls with all His ways
Reaching inward toward that mark
Each would be kind and meek
Showing the world the glory of
The One Whom each doth seek
Yes, if it were to be possible
I would brand my own heart too
So that everything I do and say
Would show my Lord to you

Let love and faithfulness never leave you; bind them around your neck, write them on the tablet of your heart.

(Proverbs 3:3, NIV).

My Kind of Bling

A sparkling colorless diamond set upon a golden band
Smooth, shiny pearls knotted onto a silken strand
A ruby as flaming red as a fire's glowing embers
A sapphire the same color as the sky in late September
An emerald just as green as the grass that springtime brings
An opal with bursting colors, a truly amazing thing
Each of these are stunning by even the strictest earthly measures
Easy it is to see why each is viewed as worldly treasure
But I've gotten to a place where I now see much more clearly
I now see the kinds of things that I should be holding dearly
Giving to the poor, gently easing someone's pains
The value in each of these only waxes, never wanes
Feeding those who are hungry, strengthening the weak
Wiping away the tear running down someone's cheek
These are the kinds of jewels that I now feel blessed to own
Each I see as treasure: each … a "heavenly gemstone"
Lending a hand to my brother when he happens to be in need
The causes of the wronged, standing up with them to plead
Reaching out a caring hand to those wandering and lost
The value in each of these far exceeds their earthly cost
No ruby, no emerald, no sapphire of a brilliant blue
Can ever shine as brightly as what these "heavenly gemstones" do
Not an opal, not a pearl, not even a diamond world renowned
Can ever exceed the worth of these beautiful jewels I've found

Then Jesus beholding him loved him, and said unto him, One thing thou lackest: go thy way, sell whatsoever thou hast, and give to the poor, and thou shalt have treasure in heaven: and come, take up the cross, and follow me. And he was sad at that saying, and went away grieved: for he had great possessions.

(Mark 10:21-22, KJV).

I Know that You Knew

How crass the sound must have been in Your ears
Did it drown out the sound of the mocks and the jeers?
For, I know You heard *then* every word I have uttered
Every lie, every slur, every harsh word I've muttered

How blinding the glare must have been to Your eyes
Did it defer from the sneers and the Pharisees' guise?
For, I know You saw *then* every deed I have done
Every sin I've committed, yes, You saw every one

How painful the betrayal must have been to Your heart
Did it lessen the agony of having Your flesh ripped apart?
For, I know You felt *then* every time that I've strayed
Every time, in every sense, at every level, and every way

How heavy the weight must have been on Your shoulders
Did it feel like the cross was laden with boulders?
For, I know all my sins were *then* carried by You
Every sin; *now* forgiven, because You paid my due

O God, thou knowest my foolishness; and my sins are not hid from thee.

(Psalm 69:5, KJV).

Meet Me Here

Here in the silence and still of the morn
I ask You to meet with me here
My soul is hungry for Your presence Lord
My spirit needs to feel You near
I open Your Word and I *listen* for You
I strive to hear every sound
Here in the silence and still of the morn
Togetherness with You I have found

Cause me to hear thy lovingkindness in the morning; for in thee do I trust: cause me to know the way wherein I should walk; for I lift up my soul unto thee.

(Psalm 143:8, KJV).

Rising up from within
To fall down my cheek
Revealing one pain
One moment, one peek
But not one is wasted
Not one that will fall
You count each one
Yes, You count them all
Evidence outward
Of what's held within
For sure pain will come
Again ... and again
But there in the pain
Your presence I feel
As you use every tear
To help my heart heal

In the Pain

As Told
By
Creation

I am so hungry for what You give

Special things You know I will see

A tiny bird in the morning sun

Its every feature designed by Thee

A cloud taking shape in a bright blue sky

Your hand, I know, guides its way

Rays of sunshine flooding the hills

As You give me a brand new day

Constantly searching, my eyes never tire

For I know I'll be blessed yet again

Your touch on creation speaks to my soul

And joy sings from somewhere within

A Fleeting Moment

When death called out my loved one's name
When love had left my side
Sorrow flooded my heart and soul
And filled me up inside
My spirit sank to the deepest deep
My heart - broke in two
But then You whispered for me to come
And spend some time with You
You told me of Your love for me
You soothed my heart's deep ache
If only for a fleeting moment
Of Your peace, I could partake
There within Your tender love
Surrounded by the sweetest Light
Sorrow had no choice but flee
Before Your gentle might
A fleeting moment, it came and passed
Then more tears, as with more pain
But ever present was Your voice
Inviting me back again
And every time I came to You
You healed me that much more
Ever so slowly and tenderly
By Your love, I've been restored

In the day when I cried, thou answeredst me, and strengthenedst me with strength in my soul.

(Psalm 138:3, KJV).

Tell Me What It Is

It does not have a fill or limit
No boundary known can restrict or hem it
No number or measure can tell its size
Or its full potential, ever recognize
Without doubt or question, it can be felt
Yet no man or woman has touched its pelt
It grows and grows when held tight
Yet grows even more when freed and takes flight
It cannot be bought, nor can it be sold
Nor can its full story be expounded or told
No power on earth, no human force
Can clone its strength or copy its course
It's here in life; and past death, it remains
It cannot be bound by stocks or chains
It is held as priceless, yet it is totally free
Tell me what it is, what you think it might be

... to know the love of Christ, which passeth knowledge, that ye might be filled with all the fulness of God.

(Ephesians 3:19, KJV).

Past the Breakers

I felt the crashing wave slam against my broken heart
In the swelling sea of pain, I could feel it tear apart
But as I weakened from the ache and trembled from the cold
I began to feel something wonderful just beginning to take hold
Though I saw the breakers forming and coming straight at me
I somehow sensed Your soothing Spirit – there – in the angry sea
Nothing could keep You from being there, from being at my side
Not a breaker, not a wave, not an ebb or rise of tide
Though the salt stung my eyes and I had nowhere to retreat
I somehow felt peace abounding; I somehow found solace sweet
For You were right there holding on; You never let me go under
You helped me let go of the ache and pain, and swim toward awe and wonder

For the mountains shall depart, and the hills be removed; but my kindness shall not depart from thee...

(Isaiah 54:10, KJV).

None Too Dirty

Jesus touched the grimy hands
He wiped tears from dirty faces
He took His heavenly heart into
Sinful men's earthly places
Jesus loved the cast-asides
The no-goods and dirt-poor
In fact, these are the very ones
The ones He came here for
Jesus gives His priceless gift
For the simple act of believing
He does not want man-made rules
To muddle the way to receiving
Jesus never said, not once
"You're too bad to have what I give you"
He never said, no, not even once
"You must be sinless before I can save you"

He is the atoning sacrifice for our sins, and not only for ours but also for the sins of the whole world.

(1 John 2:2, NIV).

When Mercy Reigned

I saw the gaping wound where the stone had hit her head
The horror on her face was clear, even through streaks of scarlet red
Her blood, it flowed, like a stream, and dripped from off her chin
As did her tears from the sorrow in knowing that she had sinned
I looked around to try to find the hand that had cast that stone
My heart shattered when first I saw ... that hand ... had been my own
Anguish stripped my breath away as my knees fell to the ground
My soul so hurt by what I'd done, I couldn't make the slightest sound
Oh how I wanted so desperately to take away her searing pain
Reversing the hands of time, putting the stone back where it had lain
Every cell within my body, every speck of my hurting soul
Begged Him to forgive me, and to restore her, make her whole
He saw the gaping wound where my stone had hit her head
The pain on His face was clear, as He washed me in scarlet red
His mercy reigned; His blood flowed free; it cleansed me of my sin
His hand wiped my tears away as He pleaded, "Don't judge again."

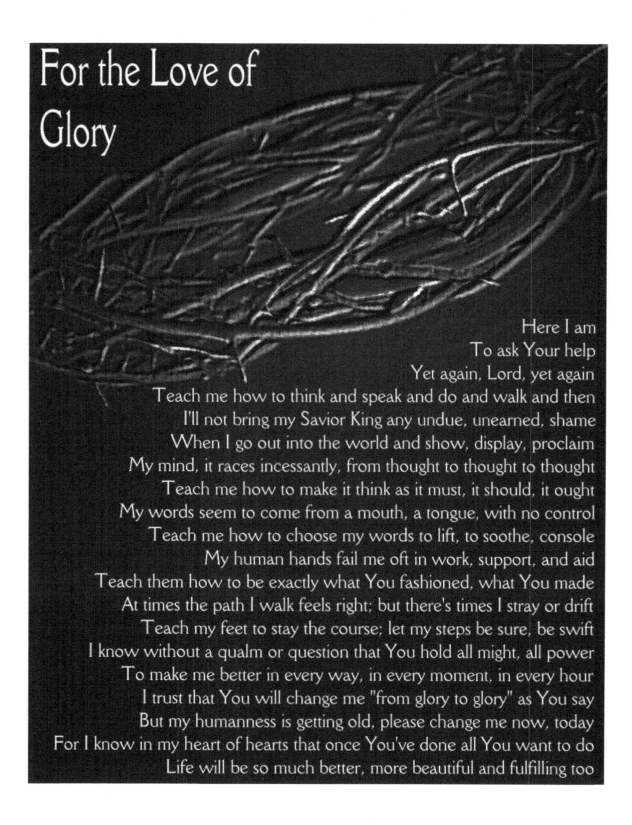

For the Love of Glory

Here I am
To ask Your help
Yet again, Lord, yet again
Teach me how to think and speak and do and walk and then
I'll not bring my Savior King any undue, unearned, shame
When I go out into the world and show, display, proclaim
My mind, it races incessantly, from thought to thought to thought
Teach me how to make it think as it must, it should, it ought
My words seem to come from a mouth, a tongue, with no control
Teach me how to choose my words to lift, to soothe, console
My human hands fail me oft in work, support, and aid
Teach them how to be exactly what You fashioned, what You made
At times the path I walk feels right; but there's times I stray or drift
Teach my feet to stay the course; let my steps be sure, be swift
I know without a qualm or question that You hold all might, all power
To make me better in every way, in every moment, in every hour
I trust that You will change me "from glory to glory" as You say
But my humanness is getting old, please change me now, today
For I know in my heart of hearts that once You've done all You want to do
Life will be so much better, more beautiful and fulfilling too

The Extra in the Ordinary

Peaceful is the soul when it senses the rustling wind
Swirls of freedom and abandon, so magically, they blend
Happy is the soul when the sunshine's touch is felt
Warmth dons the face like a soothing satin pelt
Blissful is the soul when it is treated to salty air
Lifted by the lulling waves crashing here and there
Joyous is the soul as mountain views flood the eye
Awesome splendor is freely found where stony crag meets silky sky
Stricken silent is the soul when allowing creation to sing
Praises lift without a word, as if an offering
Simply plain and ordinary is what some would say these are
They cannot see Love's promise twinkling bright in every star
They cannot hear Love singing softly in the gentle summer rain
They cannot feel the power of Love commanding wax and wane
They somehow miss the signs and wonders God graciously displays
They allow their minds to sink into the fog of logic's haze
Blessed I am to sense and taste, to touch and feel and see
Blessed I am by every one of God's blessings for you and me

Praise ye him, sun and moon: praise him, all ye stars of light. Praise him, ye heavens of heavens, and ye waters that be above the heavens. Let them praise the name of the Lord: for he commanded, and they were created.

(Psalm 148:3-5, KJV).

The Silent Blue

Dayspring, meaning the first light of day
The softness of her hues … beyond compare
I've not found any term befitting the blue
Found in the secrets of her lair
It's a purple that's been kissed with a hint of night
It's a blackness just kissed by day
It's a bluish tone no word can describe
It's a splendor no name can relay
The darkness of night is overcome by her light
Yet, of her victory, she does not shout
Instead, in the still, in the quiet, in the calm
She humbly dispels any doubt
This silent blue seems a sacred thing
The humble tithe of her magical dim?
An offering so grand I've not seen before
Dayspring's first – meant just for Him

My soul yearns for you in the night; in the morning my spirit longs for you.

(Isaiah 26:9, NIV).

Basking in Brilliance

Oh beautiful Bright And Morning Star
I want so much to be where You are
I long to stand within Your glow
I yearn Your brilliance to truly know
Oh Bright And Morning Star give Your light
Come take away the darkness of night
Immerse me in Your radiance completely
Soak into my soul, my spirit, so sweetly
Oh Bright And Morning Star let me feel it
This power, this magic, into my being, seal it
As I bask in Your brilliance, let it warm me through
Let it fill me to overflowing with the presence of You

I Jesus have sent mine angel to testify unto
you these things in the churches. I am the root
and the offspring of David, and the bright and
morning star.

(Revelation 22:16, KJV).

Cries of the Lost Soul

I am that thing you feel you lack
That thing you want to find
I am that thing you cannot name
That thing in the back of your mind
I am that thing you want to feel
That thing you want to see
I am that thing you want to hear
That thing you need to be free
These longings deep within your spirit
Are the cries of your very soul
They cannot be completely stilled
Until I have made you whole
I am that pull upon your heart
That knowing there's something more
I am that desire that reigns supreme
That thing you most long for
I am that thing that is always there
That thing that just won't leave
I am The King; I am calling your name
The King asking you to *believe*

My sheep hear my voice, and I know them, and they follow me

(John 10:27, KJV).

Undeniable

When you are filled with serene expectation
Just because of the dawn's tender light on creation
This feeling, you know, feels as right as true love
It's your soul lifting praise to its Maker above
When you are filled with intoxicating bliss
Just because of the warmth of sunlight's soft kiss
This feeling, you know, comes from deep within
It's your soul lifting praise to its Maker again
When you are filled with decadent pleasure
Just because of the richness of a sunset's treaure
This feeling, you know, you so truly adore
It's your soul lifting praise to its Maker once more
When you are filled with sheer, quiet delight
Just because of a star's ever peaceful twinkling light
This feeling, you know, is unfiltered and pure
It's your soul lifting praise to its Maker, for sure
Oh, you can deny that ... God ... is real
But you cannot deny these feelings you feel
Each one is unstoppable; from within, each pours
It's your soul lifting praise to its Maker ... and yours

Seeking the Found

I seek Your face, Your heart, Your smile; I seek Your way, Your will
I seek You without end, for though I'm full, I'm never filled
I seek Your wisdom in each loss; I seek it in each gain
I seek Your presence in sunshine, in fog, in snow, in rain
I seek Your glow with the darkness, Your shadow in the light
I seek Your guidance in each day, Your comfort in each night
I seek Your arms to lift me when I collapse under waves of pain
I seek Your hand to keep me grounded when life, its joys, regain
I seek Your touch within the breeze, Your voice within the wind
I seek Your love in the breath of life ... time and time again
I seek Your mercy when I'm wrong, Your power when I'm weak
I seek because I've found; and what I've found, I'll always seek

A Moment's While

The tree outside my window
Has needled branches hanging low
They're dancing in the morning wind
Swaying to and fro
A cold rain's softly falling
Making music on deadened leaves
Nature shares her peaceful worship
With all who dares believe
The birds lift their songs and wings
The clouds parade on by
Praises, o so beautiful
Found, right here, in the morning sky
Lift your eyes from your troubles
One moment is all it takes
Stand in worship with creation
Let your soul arise, awake
Lift your praise without a word
Let your heart sing through a silent smile
You'll find such bliss, joy serene
In but a moment's while
There's a tree outside your window
A bird singing somewhere close
Follow their lead and you can find
What your soul is needing most

Great are the works of the Lord; they are pondered by all who delight in them.

(Psalm 111:2, NIV).

Those Hands

Unknowing hands twisted stems
And wove them into a ring
Piercing thorns instead of jewels
Adorned the crown of the King
The King kept silent as those hands
Pushed the crown down on His head
As jagged edges cut His skin
Blood flowed in streams of red
Those hands that did this horrid deed
Knew not what they had done
They did not know that they had crowned
God's one and only Son
Holding back the angels' army
The King – kept still
Ten thousand legions could have come
But that was not within His will
He *allowed* those hands that *He* had made
Cause Him all that pain
For the King desired to finish His work
And forever, as Savior, reign
I have to wonder if those hands
Ever came together in prayer
Asking the One Who wore that crown
To be their Lord and Savior

And when they had platted a crown of thorns,
they put it upon his head ...

(Matthew 27:29, KJV).

A Father's Love

I paint the clouds with morning sun
I color the autumn leaves
I give the blues their changing hues
Within the deep and rolling seas
I molded each mountain from base to peak
I dipped out each valley's floor
I shaped each desert's sandy dune
I sculpted every shore
I placed the song within each bird
I silenced the still of night
I put the boom into the thunder
And the babble in each brook so slight
I softened each feather that you feel
I hardened each pebble and boulder
I tuned your senses so they could know
The comfort of a caring shoulder
I planned your face and your smile
I designed your every part
I created the pathway that love can travel
Deep within your heart
I gave you stars to wish upon
I hung them all in space
So every time you gaze at them
You look toward My face

The heavens declare the glory of God; and the firmament sheweth his handywork. Day unto day uttereth speech, and night unto night sheweth knowledge. There is no speech nor language, where their voice is not heard.

(Psalm 19:1-3, KJV).

Blessing Book

I rounded the corner of the barn
When the wind met my face
I stopped still and closed my eyes
Delighted by the air's embrace
But when I opened my eyes again
On the barn, shadows were dancing
They seemed to know the light You gave
Was meant for their enhancing
They swayed and moved so gracefully
As if in a state of bliss
Thank You Lord for giving me
Sweet treasures such as this
Thank You for these simple things
So easy to overlook
If I could, I would keep each one
In a magical blessing book

Wherefore do ye spend money for that which is not bread? and your labour for that which satisfieth not? hearken diligently unto me, and eat ye that which is good, and let your soul delight itself in fatness.

(Isaiah 55:2, KJV).

Spirit Wings

My spirit leaves my earthly body

And soars the crimson sky

I rise on wings of praise

As upon Your wind, I fly

The glow is quickly fading,

I've a few minutes, nothing more

But here within this moment

Oh, with You ... I soar

In a Darkened World

A wounded soul, hurting deeply
Feeling alone and lost
Does not fully see the weight
Of surrender's exorbitant cost
Torment slices hope's pleading call
And muffles love's desperate cry
It binds weakened wings
So that soul can no longer fly
The anguish and the agony
Hide the truth in darkness deep
Pain steals all joy and peace
As it plunders all rest and sleep
Despair pulls the curtains
So no light can enter in
It draws the blinds to hide the world
Where happiness had freely been
But there within that darkened world
Where hurting souls find false retreat
A tiny flame flickers on
A holy heart continues to beat
Christ is there; He'll not give up
He'll wait 'til that soul is ready
His flame will glow into that dark
His heart will beat ever steady
Behind the curtains, behind the blind
He holds that hurting soul
Ever working to ease the pain
And restore what suffering stole
His beating heart will never weaken
It will never give up or fail
His flickering light will not go out
It will not let the darkness prevail

See the Feeling

Just like the silent serenity
In a snow covered woodland scene
Your presence ever so gently comes in
And - oh - the peace it brings
Just like the enchanting music
Played by a calm blue sea
Your presence ever so gently comes in
And - oh - how it settles me
Just like the soothing radiance
Of a fire in a cozy hearth
Your presence ever so gently comes in
And - oh - how it warms my heart
Just like the quiet calling
In the song of the mourning dove
Your presence ever so gently comes in
And - oh - how I feel Your love

Close your eyes; see the feeling
Seek out what it is your heart is revealing
Let your senses awake to find
All the God-sent treasure to which you've been blind

If ye then, being evil, know how to give good gifts unto your children: how much more shall your heavenly Father give the Holy Spirit to them that ask him?

(Luke 11:13, KJV).

A Season of Grace

Frozen solid, bitter cold
The wind, bold in the face
The snow so white
The sky so bright
Illustrations of God's great grace
Branches bowing under the weight
Swaying with each new gust
They drop the snow
As if they know
Giving shelter is a must
Tiny footprints here and there
Songs of praise being sung
Birds take flight
To treetop height
Like ornaments now being hung
A cardinal perched high on a branch
Eyes lifted toward the sun
Warming his face
In sunlight's embrace
For a brand new day has begun
Winter is harsh, and cold, and hard
But look for its beauty … it's there
God has a reason
For this graceful season
And He fashioned it with great care

He hath made every thing beautiful in his time...

(Ecclesiastes 3:11, KJV).

My Need to See

Frost has covered every surface
With mosaic artwork in crystal form
My eyes are hungry as I wander
Just outside this winter morn
The grass is crisp; the air is frigid
Yet I feel such a need to see
Bundled up, I shake and shiver
But it's oh so worth finding Thee
Up along the ridge, I see it
Just a peak comes through the pine
Soft pink light shining upward
Today's sunrise: superb, sublime
The clouds look happy to wear its colors
Are they slowing their pace a bit?
Pastel hues in brilliant fashion
Sunrise pink, their perfect fit
My heart is filled with awe and wonder
My soul sings praise without a word
Though not a peep comes from my lips
It does not matter; I know He heard

Thou hast set all the borders of the earth: Thou hast made summer and winter.

(Psalm 74:17, KJV).

The Light in the Temple

There it stood before my eyes
Run down, quite worse for wear
But at its tired window panes
A Light glowed warmly there
I saw its tattered welcome sign
Shaped like a friendly smile
It seemed to beckon to all souls
"Come share what I have for a while"
It stood so firm on its foundation
Having been built upon the Rock
Its doors would never have to close
At the chime of any clock
And though it stood right there before me
I knew it could go at will
And take the power of the Holy Spirit
To whomever might need to be filled
Its freckled skin, scars, and wrinkles
Were what first caught my eyes' attention
But with God's help, the mirror showed
The wonder of His intention

Awake to righteousness, and sin not; for some have not the knowledge of God: I speak this to your shame.

(1 Corinthians 15:34, KJV).

Life and Breath

Every time I take a breath
I do it not alone
For so does every living thing
One breath - to all - is known

When Adam exhaled that first time
The breath of life took flight
Upon the air, the wind, the breeze
To every earthbound site

To a tiger in the orient
To a tree on an African plain
And even to a flower here
God's breath, all life, sustains

Small, I Am

Small I am within this world

As a tiny speck of dust

But each and every song I sing

You hear each one, I trust

Small I am within this world

A drop within an ocean

But everything I do, I know

You see my every motion

Small I am within this world

A grain of sand upon life's beach

But every feeling that I feel

I know You know of each

Small I am within this world

But this is not my story

This world's Maker, Ruler, King

My might ... is in His glory

My Everywhere Prayer

My legs seem so tired and weak as I take each step ahead
My courage sometimes wanes, and I must fight against the dread
I cannot see where I'll end up or where You're leading me
But I trust I'll not get lost holding so tightly, Lord, to Thee
My vision is quite clouded; I must feel my way along
Each turn I take directed by my heartbeat's constant song
The steady rhythm that it sings, it sings for only You
It tries to tell me where next to turn and what next I need to do
Help me to always hear the music You've placed within my heart
Let it soothe my fears away as each new path I start
Everywhere You take me, Lord, stay close, don't leave my side
For I'm still learning to listen to this guide You've placed inside

May the God of peace, who through the blood of the eternal covenant brought back from the dead our Lord Jesus, that great Shepherd of the sheep, equip you with everything good for doing his will, and may he work in us what is pleasing to him, through Jesus Christ, to whom be glory for ever and ever. Amen.

(Hebrews 13:20-21, NIV).

Witness of Your Glory

Fall winds blow with hints of chill
Leaves change color at Your will
Forest beauty to the fill
All – witness of Your glory
The end of summer's season now
Gold color resides on every bough
Birds fly south as if by vow
All – witness of Your glory
Potatoes, yams, and pumpkins too
Ready to harvest amidst the dew
Eyes, open wide, admiring the view
All – witness of Your glory
I don't want to miss one single way
Of seeing Fall's beauty in full display
Such gifts of color before Winter's gray
All – witness of Your glory
Thank You, Father, I treasure it so
Your love, I see, within its show
Autumn color so vivid, so You, we can know
A witness – for us – of Your glory

All thy works shall praise thee, O Lord; and thy saints shall bless thee.

(Psalm 145:10, KJV).

More to See

Capture my imagination
Lead me where You will
Let beauty, awe, and wonder
Make my heart stand still
Show me all the hidden treasures
Amongst the ordinary
Amidst those things that look the same
Show me how they vary
Open my eyes to see the splendor
Created by Your hand
Set my sight upon the small
As well as the big, the grand
A speck of dust caught on a breeze
Peacefully floating in sunrays
Or a mountain towering in a cloudless sky
Above the morning's foggy haze
A drop of rain, pristinely round
Glistening though it knows it will drop
Or a great oak's leaves in autumn colors
Proudly displayed to the very top
Show me more and more each day
I know there's more to see
Let my eyes not miss even one
Of these gifts You've sent to me

O Lord, how manifold are thy works! in wisdom hast thou made them all: the earth is full of thy riches.

(Psalm 104:24, KJV).

Our Secrets

The mix of thoughts swirling around inside
That, one-by-one, stroll through my mind
There are none that I need to cover or hide
For there is nothing to which He is blind
Moments of torture that cut to the bone
Hidden shame in the deep of my soul
These things are not private, to me alone
For God knows each one in whole
Moments of wonder and moments of awe
Moments of loss and moments of gain
Moments that have left my heart and soul raw
Moments of joy and moments of pain
My every feeling is known to Him
For He never once looks away
Whether found in the light or in the dim
All my secrets before Him lay

I know that thou canst do every thing, and that no thought can be withholden from thee.

(Job 42:2, KJV).

Far Away Nearness

You hold me close while You hold the stars
Your presence I know right well
You raise the moon to light the earth
While you sit with me for a spell
The planets dance at Your direction
The heavens, their distant dance floor
Yet while You direct their every move
You are right here with me; I am sure
The seven seas, they ebb and flow
As You command each wave of each tide
Yet here, right here, You stay with me
Right here with me, You reside
Each drop of rain upon each and every leaf
On each far away rainforest tree

You placed each one exactly where it lays
Yet You were all the while right here with me
You fill the earth; You fill the heavens
You fill my heart, my soul, and my mind
Far away nearness ... nearness far away
I need only to seek to find

Freedom's Wind

Bridled power, unbridled spirit

Some are drawn; others fear it

Thunderous hooves through whispering pine

Strength from God, his Maker divine

Servant steed, having made his choice

Yet, when he runs, he will rejoice

Nostril's flared in freedom's wind

Praises, heavenward,

His spirit

Will send

Haven

I have found a peace surpassing serenity
Tranquil - is my soul
Peace I have not seen in this world around me
Peacefulness - in its whole
Resting quietly within this peace
No care, whether small or huge
No turmoil, no tempest, no tragedy
Can move me from this refuge
For His peace He gave to me to keep
As my calm and quiet place
My harbor, my haven, my shelter too
Right here, within His grace

Peace I leave with you; my peace I give you. I
do not give to you as the world gives. Do not
let your hearts be troubled and do not be afraid.

(John 14:27, NIV).

The Message in the Morning

The rising sun casts its rich warm glow
On the blazing orange leaves of Fall
It is dusting the softest red hue on the clouds
Shaped like angels' wings, one and all
The harmony I feel as each play their part
Captivates my Daddy's girl mind
He seems to know that I am looking for Him
So He's making sure He is easy to find
A soft haunting haze is adrift far below
From the valley, it slowly ascends
Ever so steadily it makes its way
All barriers it will indeed transcend
For it knows exactly where it wants to go
It has felt the calling of its Creator
That fog in the valley will not rest until
It has become its part in something greater
A magical morning world lies before my sleepy eyes
God's message I am so blessed to see
Majesty awakens my senses to His grace
Watching nature – witnessing to me

You will seek me and find me when you seek
me with all your heart.

(Jeremiah 29:13, NIV).

Sing

Look to the signs in all of creation
Look for the proof of His power, His might
Look to the signs creation is giving
Look in the darkness; look in the light
Watch for the gifts He has so freely given
Watch for the precious, the tiny, the small
Watch for the gifts He has showered upon us
Watch for the great, the towering, the tall
Seek out the voice of creation's sweet praises
Seek out the whispers in the quiet of dawn
Seek out the voice of the praises all around us
Seek out the shouts in a thunderstorm's spawn
Glory to God, glory and honor!
Glory to God is nature's sweet song
"Glory to God", that's what its singing!
"Glory to God" from the weak and the strong
Sing from your heart the praises within you
Sing from your heart what it is that you feel
Sing from your heart your deepest thanksgiving
Sing from your heart with passion and zeal

Praise ye the Lord: for it is good to sing praises unto our God; for it is pleasant; and praise is comely.

(Psalm 147:1, KJV).

A Weakling's Week

The past several days have left me quite worn
By the weight of my grief, my joy has been shorn
The pain in my heart left me drained and weak
My light, I am sure, burned quite dim, quite bleak
Time has moved on, but the sorrow, it stays
Missing my momma just takes over some days
So exhausted, so tired, so frail I have felt
So heavy's been my cloak; so tight, my pelt
But they did their job; hidden away was my pain
Not even one eye saw my heart's crimson stain
So wearied from the week, I laid my body down
My eyes closed so quickly with no one around
But there, in sleep's dream, my tears began to pour
As I held Momma's body in my arms once more
Her soft, sweet voice came gentle to my ear
As I held her head close, cheek to cheek, so near
Awakened by my sobs, the world was the same
Drying my tears, I had to return to life's game
"Momma, I love you, somehow - more and more
Five years ago tomorrow, you walked through heaven's door
Don't you worry about me, you raised me up right
My smile will return; my light, again, will be bright
Our love was so deep that the pain must be too
But the hurt is all worth what I once had with you"

He giveth power to the faint; and to them that
have no might he increaseth strength.

(Isaiah 40:29, KJV).

Something
of
Beauty

Let the beat of my broken heart be the rhythm of the songs you sing
Let this sigh in my aching soul be the wind that lifts your wings
Let these tears that flow and flow be the water for heaven's flowers
Let my memories stack to build your new mansion's spiring towers
Let this love I still hold for you be a jewel for you to wear
Oh take this pain from losing you and make something of beauty there

Tattered Wings

Though my wings are tattered and it is hard these days to fly
I can always find the best of reasons to give it my finest try
God's gifts I've known, I confess; I've had blessings beyond compare
Some are new, some are old, and some a little worse for wear
Every creature, great and small
That has tasted from His hand
Must also know, gifts do not last
This is just how He has planned
I cannot boast of any gift
Taking credit for what He has done
But I can surely praise Him
Day and night, sun to sun
Yes, though my wings are tattered
I'll not give up one second's bliss
From knowing that His hands have made
... me ... and all of this

How Many Pearls?

Captivating beauty
Hanging from a chain
It's amazing when you think
It only exists because of pain
So smooth and so shiny
Exquisite to behold
A pearl silently speaks
Can you hear what's being told?
Things will come into our lives
That hurt us to the core
But God will use that suffering
To make us so much more
Fear and loss and tragedy
Cut into our heart and soul
But it's not our pain He wants
The finished piece is His goal
Thank You Father for the ache
For though it hurts so deep
I know You see the finished piece
The one for me to keep
How many pearls will You make
For my heart and soul to wear?
I long to see just a peek
Of the beauty collecting there

Again, the kingdom of heaven is like a merchant looking for fine pearls. When he found one of great value, he went away and sold everything he had and bought it.

(Matthew 13:45-46, NIV).

Awaiting

Abba, please, it's so dark
Let me sit a while with You
Let us sit and watch the sky
Just awaiting the fall of dew
Let me rest against Your chest
Your heartbeat I want to hear
Quietly, I'll feel Your life
As Your breath falls to my ear
Wrap Your wings lightly around
With feathers so soft and white
Cradled in Your loving arms
I can await the morning light

And I said, Oh that I had wings like a dove! for then would I fly away, and be at rest.

(Psalm 55:6, KJV).

To the Edge

The house is still and silent for it is very early morn
This brand new day now coming is still yet to be born
The nighttime hours are passing; they're growing old quite fast
Soon their cover of darkness will be left long in the past
A late autumn rain is falling softly; it's heard, but yet unseen
The melody it plays leaves me feeling so serene
There's something special about this time, about this early hour
This is where I feel the might of Your gentle presence' power
You always seem to be waiting here, no matter how early I awake
The very first glimpse of each new day, with You, I partake
Whether seeing springtime's lively green or winter's frigid white
I long to always be with You when I first take in the sight
Walk me to the edge, O God, lead me to dawn's arrival
Whatever scene awaits me there, it's being with You that has no rival
Lift the veil of nighttime dark; display what You have planned
Let me greet each day You made while holding Your loving hand

My soul waiteth for the Lord more than they that watch for the morning: I say, more than they that watch for the morning.

(Psalm 130:6, KJV).

First, Best, Forever

True love's journey can last forever.
It expects the bumps in the road;
And it willingly takes every jolt
Just to continue with its voyage.
It possesses a lasting courage
To speak and receive the truth,
All the while knowing this fact:
That the truth will sometimes hurt.
It looks past imperfections, and continues to call what it sees - a priceless gift.
True love becomes as much a part of a person as that person's very own heart.
It quickly, and with no regard for self, runs toward the opportunity to sacrifice.
True love develops its very own life force, defying the laws of space and time.
It is forever present, and, it never, ever, leaves whether times are good or bad.
True love is unique and it is precious,
Like an exquisitely faceted jewel.
Its brilliance shines the brightest
When shared between two hearts.
But it can be prized by one alone,
And can be treasure to one alone.
It has the ability to survive death.
It never considers the cost of pain.
It never calculates the cost of loss.
True love willingly pays any price
Just for the experience of that love.
True love is a blessed gift from God.
He loved us first – He loves us best,
So that now we can truly love, forever.

Whoever does not love does not know God,
because God is love.

(1 John 4:8, NIV).

A Beautiful Place

I smiled and I sang as I basked there in the sun
Then, suddenly, thunder boomed, blasting like a gun
I cowered and I cringed as the storm came roaring through
Begging for deliverance, I cried aloud to You
I staggered and I stumbled in the fearsome winds so strong
I knew I was not able to hold out for very long
I shivered and I shook from the chill of its cold rain
Desperately, I pleaded for You to release me from its pain
But when the clouds gave way to just one tiny ray of sun
It was then that I could see changes in me You had begun
I had prayed so hard and oft for You to change its course
But You knew I truly needed what was held within its force
I had been so fearful, so fragile, and so, so frail
And You knew that I would grow within its fearsome gale
I had ducked and I had dodged to get out of its way
But You knew that once it left, its gifts, with me, would stay
Now I can smile and I can laugh - though - still quite cold and wet
As I'm now much more complete and much closer to You yet
My unanswered prayers were Your mercy and Your saving grace
For here, after the storm, I'm in a much more beautiful place

What will remain of me after I'm gone?
What will my life here have meant?
Has anything I've done made a lasting change?
Or, for naught, has my time here been spent?
Whose lonely heart have I comforted?
Whose burden have I eased, and when?
Whose thoughts of others have I changed for the better?
Have I helped any outcasts fit in?
Was I ever used as my Savior's hands?
To the needy, were my feet swift enough?
Did I love the unlovable, sit with the sick
And be gentle with those who were tough?
I know my time here is measured
Though I know not the date I will leave
Oh how I hope that I will have left
A legacy that helps others believe

Wishes for a Legacy

Conclusion

Overwhelming joy, crushing sorrow, searing pain, intoxicating bliss: the range of human emotions is a truly vast and varied terrain. The turmoil of strife can completely engulf a person in its torrential flooding. The serenity of peace and tranquility can wash over a person to the point of hypnosis. To bathe in speechless wonder is one of the most powerful emotions imaginable. And then there is love! Love! Even the powers of death can't stop it from coursing through our veins!

My mind is simply incapable of wrapping itself completely around the expanse of God's love for us. He *gave* us love. But yet, He *is* Love. So then, it has to be that He gave us of Himself. Is there even one word to describe the level of perfection it would take to give a gift like that and *not* ask anything in return? God's love is perfect love. How could anyone not want to, at the very least, sample just a taste of something so amazing?

Imagine yourself being steeped in serenity. Imagine being so overwhelmed with joy that you are rendered speechless. Feeling His love, His presence, feels like this. No ... it's more, much more! Oh, if I could just describe it right! But it is bigger than thought and understanding. It is better than expression and portrayal. I cannot find *any* earthly words to do justice to this heavenly experience.

Hopefully, within the pages of this book, you have been able to sense just a touch of its consuming power and glimpse just a peek of its overwhelming majesty. My prayer for this book was that He would allow you to *feel* His love. If my prayer has been answered, *that* love, that *Love*, has captured your heart!

We have also a more sure word of prophecy;
whereunto ye do well that ye take heed, as unto
a light that shineth in a dark place, until the day
dawn, and the day star arise in your hearts

(2 Peter 1:19, KJV).

Other Works by Linda

Blessed Is My Soul

Printed in the United States
By Bookmasters